Soul Searching

THOUGHTS AND REFLECTIONS ABOUT LIFE AND NATURE

by

Shaheen Darr

*"What childhood accepts in innocence
Maturity first questions, then bows in acceptance..."*

Soul Searching
Copyright 2014 by Shaheen Darr

All Rights Reserved

This book or any portion thereof may not be reproduced or used in any manner whatsoever, without the express written permission of the publisher, except for the use of brief quotations in a book review.

For permission requests, you may email the author at
snowbrrd19@aol.com

shaheensdarr.wordpress.com

Book Interior by The Book Khaleesi
www.thebookkhaleesi.com

Other Titles by Shaheen Darr

Kismet: A Desi Rhapsody in London

The Spectrum of Life

Table of Contents

Go and Seek	*1*
Faith	*2*
Turn a Better Page	*3*
Natures Song	*4*
Make Each Day Count	*5*
Reflections on Life	*6*
Secret Door	*8*
Death	*9*
As Time Ticks On	*11*
Heartbeats	*12*
From Children	*13*
Innocence	*14*
Words	*15*
The Seekers	*17*
Nature	*18*
Fighting Spirit	*19*
Rewind Button	*20*
Board Game	*21*
No Regrets	*22*
God	*24*
Paths	*25*
Epitaph	*27*

Beacon of Light	29
Self Reflection	30
Emotions	31
Saving the Best for Last	34
A Little Closer to His Dream	35
I Said a Prayer for You Today	36
The Wave	37
A Caged Bird	38
Sea and Land	39
When Angels Cry	40
Everything You Ever Wanted	41
She Lives	42
Spirit of Child	43
The Well of Hope	44
Questions for God	45
Ups and Downs	47
Old Soul	48
Black Canvas	49
Purity	50
The Breath of Life	51
Ebb and Flow	52
Taste the Other Side	53
Inevitable	55
Leaves	56
Laughter	57
Beyond the Clouds	58
The Monk	59
Earth	60

Rain	*61*
The Village	*62*
Contrasts	*63*
Falling Drops	*64*
A Promise	*65*
Race the Wind	*66*
Hope	*67*
Disaster	*68*
A New Birth	*69*
A Gentle Touch	*71*
The Beginning	*72*
The Dove	*73*
Seasons of Life	*74*
Self Acceptance	*76*
Tilt the Balance	*77*
Puddles	*78*
Feelings	*79*
Illusionary	*81*
Endurance	*82*
Forgive Us Mother	*84*
Reminders	*86*
Prayers Answered	*87*
The Whisperer	*88*
The Present, The Future	*89*
Whispers	*90*
Why the Race?	*91*
The Dancer	*92*
Agreeing yet Asserting	*93*

The Winged Horse	*94*
The Apparition	*95*
Poems	*97*
Snapshots	*98*
Dreams	*99*
Gift of Maturity	*101*
Lies	*103*
Pearls	*104*
Adam	*105*
Wanderer	*106*
When You Left Us	*107*
About the Author	*108*

Go and Seek

Go on to seek newer pastures
Go on where no one has been before
Wake the desire in you to explore
The world lies in wait for adventures
Do not be afraid to be different
Or you will end up being indifferent
Shake those shackles loose
Come out of those walls that enclose
Let the butterfly within you fly
To roam the big wide sky
Leave that cocoon to wither and dry
Stuck on a tree, leave it to die
Go on, dare yourself and then do
Your life owes it to you
Go on and seek the new
Like a caged bird that finally flew

Faith

Faith in your Maker,
Instilled in your being the moment you take shape
A reminder that He was there is there and will always be there
When all others have long gone
Faith in friends and family
Nurtured through years of giving and sharing
They help you cope with the ups and downs of life
With helping hands, gentle words, loving touches
Faith in love, that wonderful feeling two people share
When they put their trust in each other
In sickness and in health
Till death do them apart
Faith in yourself, to live this life to the best of your ability
And make every day a special one
for you and others
so that you are never ever forgotten

Soul Searching

Turn a Better Page

If you remain who you are
And disregard the grains of sand
That trickle down the glass vial
Unstoppable like the beat of a heart
If you remember to cherish each grain that falls
Destined to never return again
And that moments, short and insignificant
Combine to make the hour momentous
If you teach that heart to love again
And resuscitate it back to life
Those feelings almost robotic
Will turn vibrant, make ambrosial
If you do all this to turn a better page
In the book of souls to secure a better ending
Then your life will have some meaning
Then my life will have some meaning

Natures Song

Can you hear the songs of nature?
The whistling wind as it flows between the trees
Making the leaves dance and sway
The splashing of the giant waves against the shore
Urging the sand to join in the play
The sounds of the animals and the birds
Singing as they go along their day
The music of the deep majestic valleys
Echoing notes they hear, as if in replay
The rippling of the clear mountain spring
Like crystals tinkling, sparkling away
The richness of a dark, starry night
Silence, yet pregnant with promises of a new day

Make Each Day Count

Live your life well, live it to the full
Make each day count, each second meaningful
Yesterday became a thing of the past
Gone, never to return, alas
Tomorrow, a new day will dawn
New hopes, new plans will be redrawn
But it is today that counts the most
Capturing the now, so nothings lost
The now shapes the past, moulds the future
Paves the way for smoother pastures
So learn to live your life to its best
To reap the fruits of the sweetest harvest

Reflections on Life

I live because I feel the joy
of waking up to another new day
knowing I can still make a difference
knowing I still have some time

I live because I breathe
breathe in the fresh air of the fields
the scent of the flowers and the grasses
nature teasing me tantalising my senses

I live because I feel you
I feel your body next to mine
the gentle rise and fall in rhythm to mine
heartbeats playing to an invisible orchestra

I live because I can worship you
give thanks for letting me see your creation
to be able to experience the gift of nature
my eyes awed at what they see

Soul Searching

I live so I too can create
sow your seeds so life can carry on
invisible magic work your spell
help it live in me, its life tied to mine

I live my counted breaths
my end written the day I was born
but before I can make my exit
I just want to live... to live

Secret Door

Wouldn't it be great if one day whilst on a walk
you stumbled upon this secret cave, cleverly hidden
as if part of the trees, part of the plants
but with a small opening visible only to you
Your heart beating fast you would watch from afar
and then your steps towards it would turn
Should you look further or should you return?
Questions while the cave continued to beckon
A door you would notice to this secret cave
Would you open it or would you leave it shut?
But maybe a golden key in it would dazzle
your hand slowly but surely this key would turn
And as the key turned the door would slowly open
What would your curious eyes see? What would it contain?
The darkness would clear and in the distance
a beautiful golden box would shine like a beacon
Unlocked, swinging open easily at your touch
all the secrets this box would possess
answers to all your questions to all our questions
life's mysteries solved, your heart satisfied

Death

He appeared from nowhere
this creature neither man nor animal
to take what he had been told to take
no one to be favoured, peasant or royal
The woman was praying, her eyes were closed
She appeared calm but her heart did race
Waves of pain shot through her body
Beads of perspiration apparent on her face
Maybe her time had come
the pain in her heart seemed to tell her so
What would her eyes see?
If only she opened them she would know
A slight breeze blew in her face
and she opened her pained eyes
You have come to take me?
Will you let me say my byes?
There was silence in that room
save her moans of pain
It reached out and touched her hand
Her life out of her seemed to drain

Soul Searching

So this is death, she thought
this is the end of my life
As hand in hand she walked
into the afterlife
She looked at her body
lying lifeless on the floor
The pain was gone now
she was to suffer no more
The creature held her hand
but walk they did not
in seconds they covered distances
and plains she knew not
Her life she had lived it well
no soul she had hurt no lies did she tell
This journey she prayed would end
in heaven and not in hell

As Time Ticks On

As time ticks on, I am learning
How much I have to do, how much I want to do
New places to visit, new interests to explore
My thirst for life just cannot be quenched
Things that once made me insecure
Now vanish, like water off a duck's back
People who once seemed better than me
Now seem just as human as me
Life has made me stronger
Depression, I just wave it goodbye
It doesn't stop to knock on my door any more
Lots of blessings, lots of good things
Have entered and made my home their own
This journey, brief though it may be
Brings new surprises for me each day
So much I have to do, so much I want to do
To enrich my life, as time keeps ticking on...

Heartbeats

Every beat of our heart reminds us of life and living
The rhythm that continues its tempo until the very end
Entwined in this rhythm are feelings of every kind
Feelings of love, feelings of joy
Feelings of hate, feelings of sorrow
Guilt about something, hurt about another
Desire to help, desire to make things better
Some make the heart feel ever so light, so pure
And some just weigh it down, heavy and not so right
But feelings have a home in our hearts, good or bad
A place safe from all prying eyes, for no other
What each one of us carries in our heart
Is the life story of a living, breathing, feeling soul

From Children

From children we learn how to speak the truth
Refreshing is their innocence, still untarnished
They teach us equality
No colour bar, no prejudice in the way they play
Their laughter is infectious, clear and loud
Fun in every little thing they try and do
Curiosity about things, about life in general
why, who, when and what constantly asked
Forgiving and quick to forget wrongdoings
Grudges and hatred still alien in their worlds
So much we can learn from our children
before age and time changes them forever

Innocence

Like the untouched pearl in the oyster
Lies hidden in the depths of the sea
Precious, pure and undiscovered
Protected from all that is dismal
Innocence is the angelic in the human
Untarnished, easily recognizable
Touching, is its simplicity
Sufficient, is its inner beauty

Words

Words of silence

He reads her lips to understand
What she says to him
In his world of silence there are no words
Only silence only peace

Words of love

His eyes reflect the love
His lips speak the words
For a moment time stands still
As he says to her again …I love you

Words of fear

Trembling with fear, her eyes wet with tears
The woman tries to stand tall, to look brave
But each word from him is like a slap
Violent… Hard… Sharp

Soul Searching

Words of hope
They listen to him as he makes his speech
Maybe he will make a difference
Could he be the one they are lolling for?
They smile as his words fill them with hope

Our words

Let words not just be words
Empty and with no meaning
Words are the voices of our souls
The interlocking links for all mankind

The Seekers

Seek the truth for therein lies freedom
No fear to stand alone, away from the crowd
Your feelings, pure, not distilled
Sifted through to release your wisdom
Choose the human over the demon
That seeks the good from the bad
And shuns all that is bad from the good
Ready for the day when you are summoned
Forget the path that leads to darkness
You will only stumble, you will only fall
No one to guide, no one to hear your call
Living a life that remains aimless
Guard the beauty that surrounds
Receive the love that abounds
Visible to eyes that look for the pure
All clear their vision, no room for the obscure

Nature

Nature presents to us beautiful views
Different snapshots of its vast terrains
A momentary earthly opportunity
To experience its immense diversity
Creatures of all shapes and sizes roam
Guided by rules that mould their destinies
In each an intrinsic code implanted
To each its place intended
Different colours blend with an invisible harmony
Reminding of seasons that lie in wait
A perfect world, as was intended
Awesome its power, its beauty splendid

Fighting Spirit

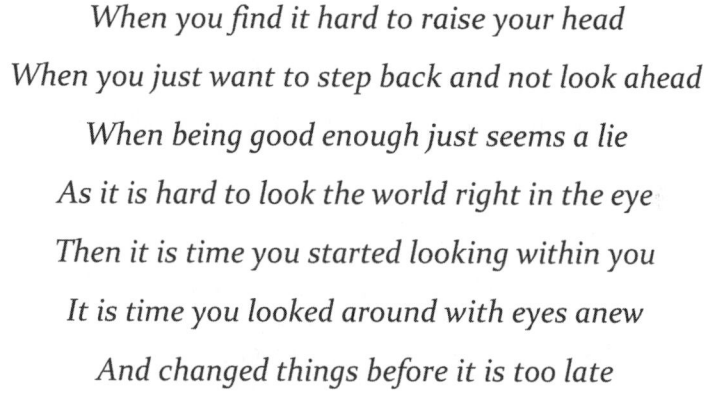

When you find it hard to raise your head
When you just want to step back and not look ahead
When being good enough just seems a lie
As it is hard to look the world right in the eye
Then it is time you started looking within you
It is time you looked around with eyes anew
And changed things before it is too late
To find that strength that lies hidden in wait
Like the phoenix rises from the burning ashes
Intact and complete, ready again to flourish
Reinvigorated to build and renew, so it can inherit
An earth that will be alive, filled with positive spirit

Rewind Button

Don't you wish life had a rewind button?
So you could go back to that moment in time
When it all started to go wrong
Have a chance to put things right, say things right
Stop the wrongs, do the rights?
But in life we are only given one chance
At that moment in time
To make up our minds, do what we can
So whatever you end up doing just remember
We cannot undo the moment that just passed

Board Game

The choices lie in wait
Playing hide and seek with me
Sometimes I see them, sometimes I don't
And some days I manage to catch one
The one that didn't get away
Changes my life for a while
And then the hide and seek begins again
More hopes, more dreams
Waiting to be fulfilled
A game waiting to be played
Life presenting itself on a board
Choose this, leave that one out
All it takes is for me to pick the right one
Have I got what it takes?
Can I get it right this time?
Can I?

No Regrets

She opens the dusty old box
Pulls out the white satin dress
The smell of dust mixed with the perfume of time
Fills the room, intoxicates her senses
Holding it to her face, she drinks it all in
This was her youth, her beauty, her passion
The hand of time has ticked many times now
Some memories too hazy to remember now
Her tired eyes glisten with tears
Life has moved on like the wave of a wand
Years have flown by as if by magic
She folds the dress and puts it back in the box
Its had its day, it's had its moment
That was then, this is now
Her lined face still beautiful in the evening light
Not one moment of her life does she want to regret
A lot she has given but a lot more she has received
She smiles as she gets up to leave the room

Soul Searching

A prayer of thanks quivers on her lips
No regrets, life, I have lived you well

God

As I look towards the horizon
Where the heavens meet the earth
Two mighty giants as if coming together as one
Mysterious, awe inspiring tricks of nature
An illusion meant just for the human eye
I watch and I ponder about it all
How it all began and how it will all end
I wonder where you are God, what you look like
A mighty human being or just the brightest light?
One day soon, though, it will happen
When the mighty giants open a path just for me
One that will lead me straight up to you
All the answers I will have to give to you
The jury, the judge all will be you
No second chance, no chance to rewind
The truth will be all revealed
Everything will be out in the open
I just hope and pray that the verdict that day
Will prove me innocent, will set me free

Paths

Was your life path chosen for you
or did you choose your own?
For some of us the choice is never ours to make
taken out of our hands decided by others
self appointed keepers of our fate
They decide who we marry and where we live
what jobs we can do and who we can see
moulded by others we are mere reflections of ourselves
our life paths hazy and so out of sight
For some of us life is a struggle
no matter how hard we try
and what we dare to dream
never seems to turn out like it should
the hand fate seems to have dealt
is never going to allow us to win
so we lose their way, lose our nerve
and some lose their lives along the way
their life paths halted before they could even begin
For some fortunate few though

Soul Searching

life's paths seem ever so clear
they know what they want, and how they want it
so they live and breathe their dreams
until they make them into realities
success bows to them, prosperity smiles at them
they show to us how the other side lives
their life paths an example for all of us to see

Epitaph

Years lived are like experiences layered on
young yesterday, today I feel so old
the eagerness and passion replaced
mellowness and sobriety now in place
The child in me is now a grown-up
some stories in books now a reality
My childhood bonds broken by death
A broken heart mended so I can carry on
My joys at bringing forth lives
sharing in their sorrows and their happiness
Beautiful memories unique to my soul
Gifts I received to be nurtured and enjoyed
Lots of ups and some downs, my life I lived it well
maybe still not to its fullest
new horizons still continue to tempt
Lots still I want to go out and explore
And when it is all gone and time is up

Soul Searching

There might still be some regrets
The epitaph brief but to the point might read
'She loved, was loving, on the whole a good human being '

Beacon of Light

Cling to hope in times of despair
It will help clear the haze your eyes can see
They say every cloud has a silver lining
Try hard enough and you can almost touch it and see
Gather Beauty, energy, bliss and qualities so pure
and use this palette to paint your life again
Use colours bright and vibrant and full of life
and as one picture is completed, start on another
Be inspired and learn to inspire others
Leave open the door and let learning walk right in
Respect others so you in turn can be respected
As in life you can only get back what you have put in
Invite God in your life so it has a meaning
Or life will seem like a road with no beginning and no ending
But do not force your beliefs on others
rather a beacon of light that draws others to you

Self Reflection

Mirror, mirror on the wall, tell me what you see?
I see you looking into me searching your soul
for answers you haven't yet found
Those deep brown eyes pools of sadness
whose depths even I cannot fathom
For others just touching my surface might suffice
but you want to dig far below and reach your roots
Some parts of your life I can now show you
why and how things were done I can tell you
But for others you will have to dive in my depths
where darkness will envelope you in its cloak
But like many others before you
you will find the light that shows you the way
And out of murky depths you will emerge
A much better person, calm and accepting
Loving others and being loved in return
those eyes that look into me will smile once again
Those pools of sadness will be content again
your study in self-reflection happily rewarded

Emotions

What complex creatures we earthlings are
Slaves to our emotions, the only feelings we truly understand
Happiness, laughter and joy the side that is uplifted
Anger, sadness, hurt and sorrow downside of life's see saw

And as we feel it all so do our bodies
every emotion reflected in the heart, the mind and the soul
Self hate manifests into bulimia; you don't feel good enough
overeating a classic cause of comfort seeking, being insecure

Pains in the neck or pains in the knee
could it be flexibility that could be an issue?
They say the heart is where the love is
could it be why the hurt lies hidden there?

The legs that take you forward, that make you move
You let them stagnate, you made them stop
Get them going again, keep them walking
Make them go freely where they once loved to go

Soul Searching

Knees and hands, fingers and toes
Joints to be moved or arthritis will befriend them so
Pains in the stomach, problems of indigestion
Or worries and insecurities bubbling around unseen?

Headaches and migraines, barometers of stress
remind you to let it go, give it a rest
Acne and boils two unwanted guests
send them packing with the anger and the stress

Being sensitive makes you so insecure
Shy and withdrawn the whole world seems so against you
The immune system just cannot fight the germs
Colds and coughs soon become the result

Stand up for yourself, learn to speak that mind
the more open you get the happier you will get
Is hate eating the good in your soul?
Did they say what they should never have said?

Or did they dare to do what they never should have done?
Begin to forgive, learn to accept
What cannot be changed will into a cancer manifest

Soul Searching

Free your heart, free your soul, just learn to let them go

Meditate to calm that restless mind
Calm and focused it will learn to become
and as the words of the mantra begin to flow
So will the thoughts taking over the show

Replace them with the new, replace them with the good
each breath a new being as if being bred
Give thanks where thanks is due
Live each day like it is your last

Surround yourself with the good and the pure
Count each blessing that has come your way
Your face will glow, your being uplifted
Disease will exit starved without negativity

Listen to the signals your body gives to you
Learn to breathe, learn to laugh
Learn to give, learn to love
in return your body will give you the best

Soul Searching

Saving the Best for Last

Journeys made, distances travelled
She searched to find herself
And fill a gaping void
No human ever fulfilled
Only nature satisfied her soul
Nourishing her parched eyes
With beauty, unparalleled
Over which no man had control
As she watched the sky so vast
The heavens watched her back
Only a fraction, yet seen
They were saving the best for last

A Little Closer to His Dream

With each step he takes, the journey gets shorter
The peak of the mountain a little bit closer
He holds on firm, afraid of the sheer drop that waits
Where many have fallen, victims of their fates
Something spurs him on, keeps him climbing
Stops him from giving up, keeps on coaxing
Many a years for this, he has journeyed
He has a dream to fulfill, a desire to succeed
Now is not the time to give it up and leave
And forget what it was that made him believe
He is getting a little closer to his dream
The time is getting nearer for his to redeem

I Said a Prayer for You Today

As I knelt down today before the Lord

Thanked Him for all the blessings of my day

The food on my table, the love of my family

The ability to live my life, my way

A small face I saw on TV came into my mind

A child hungry, a child starved

With eyes, huge, full of unsaid words

Eyes that seemed to fill up the whole face

Despair and pain-filled pools of innocence

My hands lifted up in prayer, my eyes filled with tears

This is to let you know, even so far away from you

You are never, ever forgotten

From the depths of my heart and my soul

I said a prayer for you today

The Wave

The scene was perfect, as if out of a painting
The sun lent its languid warmth to the ocean waves
As the palm trees swayed to unseen music
Waves rose and fell on the soft sandy beach
Like the gentle breathing of a sleeping giant
The deceptive scene was soon to change
When a menacing wave made its way towards the shore
No child, man or woman was spared
Many died, many hurt, many lives forever changed
The painting destroyed, now lay tattered and torn
Only screams and wails from it could be heard
Human life was never this dispensable
The day the tsunami vent its wrath upon earth

A Caged Bird

I can see a world free to do what it wants
People walking by, without a glance at me
Some stop with smiles on their faces
Making sounds, coaxing me to speak
I watch them all and wish my eyes they would read
The hurt, the pain a caged bird might feel
My wings clipped, my freedom curtailed
What was it like to fly, with other birds just like me?
Over the tall trees, then swooping down below
The wind of freedom in my face
Never to see it all again, to feel it again
My wings of freedom, now just a dream

Sea and Land

The ocean waves call to me from a distance
A wild animal as if caged, its will not allowed to be
The tide is out, the sea bed free for me to walk on
A carpet of sand spread out under my bare feet
Picking little shells, watching the crabs scurry past me
I walk miles on it, the sun beating down upon me
Slowly, the waves start making a comeback
Each time the water gets higher and then even higher
And then draws back as if by an invisible string
I play games with it each time it comes towards me
Allowing the waves to touch me, to caress me
The power of the tide gets stronger
The waves noisy as if annoyed at me
Wanting to claim their land back again from me
No human allowed to walk on this sea bed
Home of the waves alone, home of the mighty sea

When Angels Cry

When human beings grow greedy
And want to grab all that they can see
No thought of the poor man that yearns
With a hungry stomach that churns
When human beings don't help the poor
Those that toil and those that labour
All they do is to turn a blind eye
And never ask the reasons why
When human beings begin to hate
By colour and race they discriminate
Divisions grow, distances widen
Minds get set, hearts begin to harden
When human beings stop to care
For those who are in despair
That's when angels cry in sorrow
For a world that has no tomorrow

Everything You Ever Wanted

Everything you ever wanted, but could never have
Things looked so near, yet remained so far
Like a ghost, of human body devoid
Knows not how love can be enjoyed
Fate's plans, no one dare rent asunder
What is once written, sets itself in stone
Finding your path in that stony maze
Is like being in a fog thick with haze
Many seem to have it all, lives of plenty
A piece of paradise as if given to them for free
They flaunt it all, like peacocks in splendour
Strutting about no thoughts for humans lesser
You watch and give yourself the hope
All that glitters is never gold
Yearnings for now can stay unsatisfied
Hopes saved for a new world, pure, not tainted

She Lives

Who says she has gone?
Out of our world, forever withdrawn?
Never to be seen ever again
Flown yonder into the vast horizon?
Try looking for her with my eyes
And prepare for a pleasant surprise
For she lives amongst the flowers
The wind echoing her gentle laughter
She plays in the green fields
Invisible, not wanting to be revealed
She lives amongst the trees
Reborn amongst nature's bounties

Spirit of Child

Born too soon, eager to see the world
Vulnerability chosen over the safety of the womb
Small, frail child with the strength of an adult
How did you survive those days of turmoil?
Each day seemed to be your last
A mother's yearning fulfilled only from afar
The angels meanwhile played with you as you slept
Little smiles flickering on your bonnie face
Days of waiting finally gave respite
as my child grew stronger and stronger
my prayers seemed to have been finally answered
long live the spirit of my little child

The Well of Hope

Another day begins, long before the sun shows its face
A bare footed woman treks for miles on rough terrain
The journey she makes, is for water
So her family can feed, her child can drink
The woman walks on, as if one mesmerized
Treading the well known, the well worn, dusty path
A burden on her shoulders, not one she can easily forfeit
Each drop of her sweat she barters for each drop of precious water
Her opponent, the vast dusty earth, hard and arid
She looks up, tired eyes searching for respite
Dried out clouds offer her no hope, no shade
The sun's rays glare back from the bluest sky
The woman treks on, wiping her hot sweaty brow
A prayer escaping from dried, thirsty lips
Hoping she is in time for a well that is full,
If only she knew, no answers to her prayers she will ever get
The world will only get warmer,
Until her last well of hope dries to its last drop...

Soul Searching

Questions for God

God, I finally meet you in person
or should I say in spirit?
I have limited time I am told
to ask you a few questions
so mustering up all my strength here goes...
What was the reason you sent me to earth?
What unfinished business did I have to tend to?
Mistakes I made at every point in life
sometimes lost my way, didn't know where to turn
Prayed sometimes, always waiting for some sign from you
I saw greed, selfishness, cruelty and hate
wondered why people could hurt each other so
wanted it all to stop, for you to put things right
So that there would be good things for all
No man to want, no child to cry
volcanoes erupted, rivers burst their banks
people lost their homes, lost their families
their tears flowed and in their despair
they prayed to you, they didn't lose hope

Soul Searching

They got up to try their hand at life again
Where did your world go so wrong?
Why will it all have to be destroyed
before it can get better again?
Why will we all have to taste death
before we can learn to live again?

Ups and Downs

So full of happiness, life seems so complete
Every day eagerly awaited, anticipation mounts
Beauty in the face, body so voluptuous
In her book she writes her own pages
Until she finds the book of life
The first thing she reads, fills her with dread
Whatever goes up, has to come down
Sadness is the sister of happiness
Age the other side of beauty
Forever the optimist, she shuts the book
Meanwhile the hand of time, the faithful servant
Slaves, be it day or night, winter or summer
She goes to the book and opens it once again
A wise old face peers back, the youth replaced
She reads it again, the book that had been shut
And as she reads, she starts to understand
Life is full of ups and downs
the good follows the bad
The secret lies in making the best of what you have
At the present moment of your life....

Old Soul

I look at your face
So young and unlined, the face of a child
But your eyes reveal the wisdom you hide
The wisdom of an old soul
The words that find their way through you
The actions that reveal the inner you
Your patience when others are losing theirs
Words of comfort in times of distress
No room for anger in that tender heart
A gentle hand to calm when things are bad
Wise beyond those tender years
The more I look at you, the more I understand
It is the cycle of life that has made you so
An old soul found its way to you

Black Canvas

Blank canvas about to be transformed
Feelings, emotions ready to be drawn
Excitement running high, energy unleashed
The blank white to be colour treated
The first coat of brush dips deep
the deepest of red stains the white
Fingers holding the brush paint their magic
Feelings in colour do their dance
More colours on the palette beckon
The green comes next and then the yellow
A scene now slowly seems to form
There's trees and plants the brush reveals
The blank canvas unrecognizable now
Myriad of colours adorn it now
An autumnal scene painted to perfection
A part of nature brought to life

Purity

Purity lies in nature still untouched
The rippling mountain spring, crystal clear
Like a mirror revealing all that lies within
Purity lies in children still uninfluenced
In their world, they share and they love
No colour bar, no prejudice can enter in
Purity lies in the air of the countryside
It flows unpolluted amongst the trees
Light and free, no fumes to weigh it down
Purity lies in some human beings
A breed apart, walking amidst the crowds
Like angels, invisible amongst us all

The Breath of Life

Once Earth revolved around in space
Just wilderness on its vast surface
A planet so desolate, so lonely and so dark
No human, no animal not even a lark
And then a miracle took place
That changed the fate of the human race
The hand of God touched the dead earth
And filled it with colour and re birth
Animals roamed and birds flew
Fish swam in seas so blue
Creatures that crawled and crept
Found a home on earth that had slept
Plants and trees and flowers so bright
Grew tall and flourished in the sunlight
Human beings were given a new life
When God breathed into them the breath of life

Ebb and Flow

Meandering routes
Of fun and discovery
Or struggles through a maze?
Life's paths have no fixed outcomes
Set for us to choose
Like the rose befriends the thorn
Entwined together as they grow
Or the lover who pines
For love long moved on
Like the chill of the cold wintry night
Replaces the warmth of hot summer days
Life gives back what it takes
Like the eternal tide
We live in a cycle of ebb and flow

Taste the Other Side

Hard times for us?
Now taste the other side
While we have plenty
they have nothing
We throw away our food
they eat scraps
Discard our clothes?
They wear rags
Shop till we drop?
Nonsense in their world
Drink and drive?
They are thirsty, their wells dried
Our house is our palace?
Their home is under the stars
Are we warm and cosy?
They live without a blanket
Make our voices heard?
They are silent, no one to listen
Our hard times,

Soul Searching

The credit crunch? less shopping?
Their hard times?
Poverty, drought, famine... a living death

Inevitable

Life is made for living
every moment a role is being fulfilled
Sometimes it's a parent, sometimes it's a child
maybe a ruler maybe a wife
Lots of roles lots of times
Living, breathing human lives
No one knows when it will end
today, maybe tomorrow?
A mystery no one can solve
a gamble no one can win
Meanwhile the sinister watcher
cloaked in a shroud of darkness
eyes awake, never one to sleep
watches in amusement
at the hustle bustle of mankind
how quickly they would all come to a stop
their roles quickly forgotten
If they remembered
the only inevitable thing remaining
is death .... is me

Leaves

Leaves come in every shape and form
perfectly designed by the invisible designer
busy at work his artistry weaves its magic
dipping in the most colorful palette
The trees empty and bare they would be
if leaves did not adorn them so
rustling and dancing in the wind
playing to that invisible orchestra of nature
The birds and the animals hide in the leaves
sheltered from the man below
in their bosom they nurture their young
songs of nature their only lullabies
Once in abundance leaves then have to go
the cycle of life touches them too
their breath is part of our planets breath
in a chain we are all interconnected
How important are leaves to us
their beauty for all of us to see
delicate, colourful and intricate
leaves, the Invisible artist's creation

Laughter

Life can be hard to live sometimes
in the daily rush to do this and do that
let us not forget to use the free gift we have
the gift of laughter
When times are hard, when all you can see is the dark
It is easier to close your eyes and just give up
Start looking for the rainbow
That brightens even the greyest sky
Even in moments so sad
find something that will make you smile
Remember times that make you happy
Remember the clown that made you laugh
Make this journey a memorable one
Not just for yourselves but for others too
And do not forget to use your free gift
The gift of laughter

Beyond the Clouds

Fluffy balls of white cotton float across the blue sky
Carried by the wind, changing shapes as they fly
I watch them as they complete their daily journey
Never allowed to stop, be it sunny or even rainy
But what my eyes can see is not really the end
It is but the beginning, where it all transcends
Where the answers do lie, where truth does await
Who we are, why and what was the reason to create
The worlds that turn, the galaxies that rotate
Like us they obey and yet they too do wait
Thousands of years, they have seen it all happen
No sign of hell as yet and no sign of any heaven
No answers yet to these secrets are we allowed
The mysteries remain of what lies beyond the clouds

The Monk

The monk sits in meditation
in the ultimate pose of relaxation
Cross legged, his eyes closed
mantra on his lips, serene is his pose
Shutting out the sounds that break the silence
Peace and harmony on his countenance
As he controls the lengths of his breaths
he takes on the stillness of death

Earth

Earth, a lit up, rotating, revolving, body

Given the power to nurture, to create

Mother to all forms of living organisms

A home, vast, beyond our imagination

And yet, in the grand scheme of things

Where galaxies shape and form

It exists alone, lonely and miniscule

Rain

A blue expanse, the sky was like the sea

No white cloud floated on that surface

The land sweated under the dry heat

Thirsty trees stood like giants with heads bowed

Respite seemed a long way coming

As hot became even hotter

And then darkness claimed the blue sky

From nowhere, it sent dark clouds as a cover

The atmosphere became heavy and expectant

Claps of thunder announced a welcome arrival

Drops of water fell on ground, parched

Finally, it rained and the earth drank its fill

The Village

The laughter of children echo all around

Scaring the little animals into the trees

Scolding mothers sigh to their wasted words

As they cook on the outdoor fires

Men tend to their farms

Tilling earth that is ripe and fertile

The elders warm their aching limbs in the sun

Singing songs of days gone by

Simple lives, simple needs,

A little fulfilling a lot, no room for greed

Human beings and animals, one with nature

Just how nature meant it to be

The village, pure, untouched and carefree

Contrasts

Contrasts

Show us there is good

Where there is evil

Show us there is joy

Where there is sadness

Show us there is abundance

Where there is poverty

Show us there is hope

Where there is despair

Show us there is life

Where there is death

Falling Drops

She watches the dew drops on the young leaf

Perfect clear drops resting on the soft green

She tastes the water, cold, yet unpolluted

Holding the essence of that fresh morning

When memories overwhelm and sadness overcomes

Drops start to fall from her eyes so sad

The dew absorbs them and makes them as one

Leaving its own purity untouched

It soothes, as it dilutes the salt of the earth

A Promise

A rainbow makes a gloomy day seem bright

A heavenly sign maybe

That one day all wrong will be made right?

On a day, wet and so dismal

The sun comes out to make this promise

A dark and dreary sky to make so colourful

Race the Wind

My energy abounds, my feet want to flee

Nothing can hold my spirit down, today I feel so free

I want to embrace life, hold it in my arms

My heart races, but I feel so calm

The outdoor tempts, calls out to me

"Come out to me, come and play with me"

Like a child with a heart open to receive

I look at the trees sprouting with new leaves

Spring is in the air, everything's fresh and beautiful

Apple blossom trees, bright and colourful

Sway in the wind, dance to natures tune

Their little flowers cover the ground that afternoon

I want to fly like a bird, I want to laugh and sing

Today I want to race; I want to race the wind

Hope

Hope had left her heart

A place too dark for it to survive

Gloom soon found a way in

Within her left to thrive

Forlorn, one day she found a rosary

Wiped its black beads so dusty

Prayed on it the name of her Lord

To guide her out of her misery

The angels wiped her tears that flowed

Helped her stand and face the world

She opened the door she had closed

hope walked back into a home that shone

Disaster

What makes disaster strike?

What makes it target the poor, already at strife?

Tested to the extreme

They struggle as if to stay upstream

Images of their poverty, hunger and their thirst

Shown to all, in public broadcasts

Their tears, their cries, their bodies bloodied

Lying on the streets, dead, untended

As new tests for mankind on earth will continue

Man will help man, do all they can, to each other rescue

Working through the day and through the night

In some small way, struggling to make things right

A New Birth

Like the candle burns bright just before it dies

One last flash hoping to regain its dimming light

Leaves too perform a last dance

And herald a new season with flamboyance

Winds remind them of colder days to come

Gently coaxing so they willingly succumb

And let go of mothering branches that held them so

That saw them bud, that saw them grow

Defiance takes the reins, time to take over the show

The gentle, the shy leaf to exist no more

No more to be the same, to be so uniform

Time to bring out the self, to just perform

Out come the reds, out come the maroons,

Like the butterfly springing from the cocoon

No time to stay in the shade

Soul Searching

They even wear gold for this parade

Everywhere you look, colour abounds

It makes you gasp it makes you turn around

the show is on, watch this one before it goes

This is their last dance in death's throes

Fallen they lie in their thousands

At the feet of the silent giants

Their red colour taints the dark earth

Their death prophesises a new birth

Soul Searching

A Gentle Touch

Why have we become so hard, so cynical

what has made our hearts turn into stone

A parting curse as if whispered by king Midas

His final touch for us unsuspecting mortals

Searching, seeking what we cannot find

Traversing life's labyrinth, long and so dense

Sometimes we find what we seek, but not for very long

Before the desire for more starts to rekindle the mind

Travelling along these paths, changes start to appear

The softness goes; the human learns to be unkind

Each to his own, each one vying for the grapevine

No one wants to care, no virtue that seems to endear

The world, its people have lost so much

Time to wake and time to change

Time to care and time to nurture

Time to give back a gentle touch

The Beginning

Where I came from, colour and race don't mean a thing

Bodies don't hold you down, the mind is free and everlasting

The road of eternity spreads out long and unending

Trees and flowers of every shade enhances every setting

Well-wishers float around with greetings warm and welcoming

No worries of wealth and no health warnings

The ending will bring mankind back to its beginning

That will be my home, I will go back to the all knowing

That's where I came from, where my life will find its true meaning

The Dove

The clouds of dust cleared and through the burning rubble

I saw destruction straddling the once peaceful land so green

What had taken men years to build and to nurture

Now lay broken, twisted and unrecognisable

I heard cries of men, women and of children

Cries that questioned, cries that made me tremble

Lives had no meaning that fateful day

When destruction reigned as king for that day

As my dazed eyes looked at this scene so dreadful

A speck of white I saw on the horizon

A dove, untainted and untouched flew regardless

Its journey had to go on even as the world wept

A peaceful, silent messenger flew above the rest

I wished I too could fly to where she flew

I wished I too could be oblivious to it all

Just like the dove

Seasons of Life

New beginnings, a spring like season arrives

Human birth, a seedling in the garden of life

Childlike innocence, eyes crystal clear, untouched

Taking first steps, discovering what life is all about

Discovery continues, awareness abounds

Summery days get fuelled by the fire of youth

Too many distractions leave no time for reflection

The passing of time just goes unnoticed

All summer days, have to come to an end

When the winds of autumn start to blow

The soul now starts to reflect, on times gone by

Bodies that never tired, now ask for help

The winter chill never felt this cold before

Bones never felt this weak before

Soul Searching

the soul, too tired to remember its past

Now sits in the dark, awaiting a new chapter

Self Acceptance

Self acceptance can grow in the rockiest of gardens

It might take a while to struggle through

But if the root is strong, the will is firm

It will show itself, resilient and strong

As you recognise your qualities

The abilities that make you who you are

You will learn to fall in love

With whoever you see in your mirror

Through it all the beauty of the inner you

will help affirm the uniqueness of you

your life meant just for you, and no other

Tilt the Balance

Remember to pray when the sun hides and darkness falls

In the lonely night you will hear your conscience call

Not one to turn back, it will knock, a knock quite austere

While tossing and turning the silence will force you to hear

Pray for a new dawn so you can make a difference

So you have enough time to do your penance

A few more chances you might get, to turn over a new leaf

Before your time is up and your life taken as if by a thief

So tonight remember to pray

You might just tilt the balance your way

Puddles

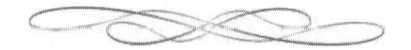

Rained over a land, dry as could possibly be

Clouds emptied of water, float light and free

Children splashing, jumping in puddles

All around, spread sounds of laughter and giggles

Single or in groups, only one thought in mind

To have fun, more victims to find

No heed, no listening to scolding adults

Blame it all on this rain, this is the result

The sky now clear, no sign of any thunder

No more laden clouds spilling any water

The thirsty land drinks it all in

Like a sponge the water soaks right in

The trees sway, making the leaves dance

Enjoy this scene; you might not get another chance

Feelings

Do you feel what I feel?

Do you see what I see?

Humans being ill treated

Wrongs being committed

Brothers stand against brothers

On the land of their forefathers

Where trees once swayed with fruit

Now blood feeds every root

Was there ever a gentle side of man?

Or is this how it first began?

History repeating itself

Cain striking the first blow

And starting the whole show

Egos feeding the ravenous self

Soul Searching

Fighting, killing, screaming, grabbing

In the end, nothing gained, lying useless, just dying

Illusionary

Passing clouds like fluffy gentle giants

Change shapes as they lightly drift by

Seemingly near, yet remaining so far

Keeping an earthly watch from the distant sky

They reveal an illusionary horizon

Where the earth seems to meet the sky

Making the traveller hopeful

Of distances that he could fulfil

On approaching close, nothing seems to change

The sky still aloof, keeping the same range

The earth and the sky destined to remain apart

Beating together with two different hearts

Endurance

Why are there stumbling blocks on every route?

Testing man's endurance before any seed sees fruit

How much more can the dashing of hopes

Be borne until someone throws in a rope

Human beings do enjoy blessings on this vast earth

But like all things the price they pay is dearth

Showing up in all corners, playing hide and seek

Like a gremlin, taunts, teases those that are meek

We carry on regardless for that is what is right

Never to give up, never to lose the fight

For that's what we have been sent here to do

One living planet chosen for us to journey through

When the day of questions looms up close

Let's pray we can be amongst those

Soul Searching

Who can tell their story with honesty

To join the ranks of those fit for glory

Forgive Us Mother

As I lie down on the carpet of soft green grass

I look up at the branches of the oak looming above me

Her protective branches hide the clouds as they pass

Playing hide and seek as if in the clear blue sea

And then I see the fallen leaves of yesteryear

Dry and crisp, lifeless at the feet of their tree

Death has not spared them it would appear

Its finger has touched them as meant to be

Sadness overwhelms me as I think of earth

A virgin once, young and full of promises

Lush, fertile, rich, and so full of worth

Waiting to grow, waiting for new enterprises

Soul Searching

Through the years as men became corrupt

Wanted more and more, gave less and less

All that was natural on Earth did they disrupt

She started to change, she began to stress

Under her silent surface, her blood began to boil

No more tears, now they started to dry

Feeling ravaged she only felt recoil

It was as if she gave up and wanted to die

I put my face against the soft grass and cried

Mother earth, forgive us, give us another chance

Only silence around me, but the wind did sigh

My cheeks were wet as the sun set in the distance

Reminders

We learn something new each day

Reminders of how little we know

Lessons from one lifetime never enough

How many rebirths to undertake?

Gathering, coveting, seeking, collecting

The heavens watch in amusement

As we strive to conquer it all

No strength, no power on anyone bestowed

To grasp it whole, to have it all

To each, the share intended

No more, no less, handed

Prayers Answered

Some have their prayers answered in a year, in a month, in a day

Not for him this privilege, only a long delay

He waited for years for the heavens to hear

To waive the haze that made his life so unclear

Just two women on his either side

The woman who bore him and his would be bride

They never lost hope, they kept vigil

Even when his days ahead seemed so dismal

The sun shone the day he headed the queue

When it was finally his turn to get through

Misty eyed, the tired man looked around, exhausted

In front of his determination, even the heavens had relented

The Whisperer

So who is this other that lives within us?

The one that makes us question and doubt

And shows us what hate is all about

The one that whispers to distract when in prayer

And causes the hope in the human to shatter

The one that makes the glitter in the gold

Overshadow everything else in the world

So who is this other that lives within us?

The twin we all have to learn to harness?

The Present, The Future

She walked the well traversed routes

Each step stirring the still world of memories

Wrapping themselves around her

She heard them, she saw them, she felt them

Some hazy, too distant to remember

Others vibrant and so alive

Eyes flowed for times that had flown by

Taken with it loved ones, no longer beside her

Little hands clasped hers as she reminisced

New lives reminded her time never stood still

It had to make way for rebirth

Tugging at her hand, urging her to move on

The child was the present, the future

No place in the now, their time spent

Her memories disappeared into their silent world

Whispers

Amongst the babble where sounds reverberate

And words remain indistinct

Gentle voices float weightless and so weak

Becoming whispers, too gentle to claim any ground

No one hears the words uttered

Only the strong rising amongst the rest

Silenced, unheard, unnoticed

The gentle sink, drowned in the din

Why the Race?

Why the distaste, why the disdain

To deliberately disregard values of old

Why let go of wisdom that age nurtured

Replacing it with flimsy distractions

Why let those sturdy roots go unwatered

Watching the stooping branches wither and die

Why the calculated moves to reach forward

Ignoring those that lay the founding grounds

Why replace all that was built with the heart

With something that exists without a soul

Why the desire to live life so fast

When death follows so closely behind

The Dancer

As light shone on a stage well set

Silence fell swiftly upon the crowds

The music played a haunting melody

To welcome a vision in white

She started to dance to a crowd, mesmerised

Musical notes translated into steps of dance

Made them sing, made them cry

Took them to a world, beautiful but unreal

They gasped, as the music came to a stop

Amidst cheers of encore, she bowed her farewell

The curtains fell, the vision vanished

The show over

Agreeing yet Asserting

Finding the right words to say yes

Freedom to voice an opinion

Inner feelings given vent

Right to say yes when all others say no

Mustering the strength to confirm

Attesting and approving

Trusting and believing

Insisting and assuring

Opting only for conviction

Not doubting but maintaining

Supporting and stating

A soul's right for existing

Soul Searching

The Winged Horse

As darkness wraps its cloak around the land

Animals vanish hurriedly to their resting grounds

The stars twinkle from the velvety sky far above

As if signalling for a miracle about to happen

The sound of wings fills the dark night air

A mystical horse, pure as a pearl, white as snow

An angel from heaven paying us an earthly visit

Silhouetted, proud against the moonlit sky

It stands and watches and takes in the view

No one, to witness this scene but one pair of eyes

A child watching from his room up high

His face so bright, his eyes wide with delight

And as he watches it is time for the horse to move on again

Its wings rise, ready for its flight back home again

It vanishes swiftly as it came

Never to be seen again

The Apparition

On waking from a troubled sleep

The man looks across the room

In front of his eyes, a figure begins to form

A faceless shape, he has no idea of whom

Frightened, he tries to converse

But no words come out, only a gasp, words, without

The silent apparition sails up close

Until the frightened man squeaks

'Why are you here?' this is not your world!

Go back; it must be someone else you seek!

A silent answer the apparition gives in return

No words spoken, yet all understood

'You are in my world now, not I in yours

Awake to me, but asleep to the world

The man looks at his bed in horror

Soul Searching

And sees himself sleeping in peace

Feelings of sadness overcome him

As from his body, his soul begins its release

Poems

Through poems inner thoughts find an outlet

Expressions of love silently professed

The pen takes over what the tongue cannot say

Words, thoughts take a life of their own

Ballads of old, stories sung about love

Epics like Iliad, so long, took a whole book

The pen's flow can write a free verse

or rhyme a word at the end of every line

A Narrative is born as a story unfolds

or a Lyric appears to express inner thoughts

Death could inspire the writing of an elegy

An urdu ghazal if the poet is a true romantic

Sometimes a couplet, other times an acrostic

What a expressive, rich form of writing this is

Poems, the heartbeat of creative souls

Snapshots

Wonderful memories, captured in time

Each snapshot has its own story to tell

Silent, with no need for spoken words

But so rich is this unspoken mode

Childhood captured from the moment of birth

Gradual transitions into adulthood

Revealed on the turn of each album page

People long gone still watch and smile

Captured on snapshots, they still live on

Each moment, a priceless treasure

Places, countries visited with them

On snapshots, the stories continue to tell

Laughter still can be heard

Ghosts still continue to live

Dreams

The waves of sleep take over slowly but surely

my tired eyes losing their struggle to stay awake

I am now entering that other world

the world of our dreams

I can fly from place to place here if I want

countries are no barrier here

Strange people I meet here

some so strange and some so wonderful

They take different shapes and forms

in this.... my dream wonderland

People long gone come and say hello

sometimes looking happy and sometimes so sad

Then they leave me and go away again

leaving me playing hide and seek again

Sometimes it is dark as the night

Soul Searching

and sometimes It is daylight

There are times I feel so light and free

and other times my feet heavy as can be

Weighed down especially when I want to flee

flee from some strange unfamiliar being

This world unfolds a new drama for me every night

some new game it sets out for me to play

As the spell of the night wears off

I wake up again and wonder....what a dream!

Gift of Maturity

They opened books that were closed years ago

Taken out of storage, long forgotten archives

Turned pages fragile as if reluctant to show

Half told stories that had shaped their lives

Eyes glistening with held back tears

Now found relief as droplets found an outlet

Memories of stifled youth over the years

Finally cleaned the slate, repaid the debt

It was time to move on and review

What life had on offer for the moment, for now

But passing years had also added their value

On them both, a gift of maturity bestowed

Soul Searching

Loving families, blessings of friends

Children that looked upon them with hope

Much more they received in exchange for what they lent

That helped them smile, that helped them to cope

Their story was in no way unfinished

It had new chapters to add

Roles to be fulfilled, goals to be accomplished

Misery replaced with visions of good times ahead

Lies

Peel away those layers that cover your inside

Let me see what it is that you really hide

Leave the acting for those that can be fooled

Let my world discover the reality that once ruled

Get in touch with what was once so real

Let us not live in this world, so fragile

For one day, just one day, see through my eyes

For one day, just one day, come face to face with your lies

Pearls

The words that flowed from your mouth

The pearls of wisdom, I gathered and held so dear

Helped me through times when trials grew tall

Tried to tower and take over, a spirit so young

It was then that I searched inside my heart

Each wise word, carefully, took out of its safekeeping

Read it and understood it and made it my guard

The pearls you left for me, pure and untainted

Today I gathered up close, my memories of my past

And as I missed your presence so dear

I wanted to let you know, I still wear that necklace of pearls

Adam

Innocence surrounds you as you play

A new game of interest emerges every day

Eyes wide, absorbing natures' abundance

Fearless, brimming with confidence

A big wide world lies silently in wait

Each year to unveil a whole new state

As in strength you grow

With each new tomorrow

Now you, the child then you, the adult

My prayers only for peace, never for tumult

The essence of mothering years to culminate

Into a man that others hasten to emulate

Wanderer

Wanderer, let those tired feet come back home

Close the door to that curious brain

That won't let you stop and pause.....

New experiences will play hide and seek

Like mirages in the sweltering desert

Entice the thirsty traveller to lose his way

Let that tired body find comfort

In the loving arms that wait with patience

Give those seeking eyes some solace

Let them close in a sleep so deep

Come back to the familiar

To what you already know

Where you get what you see

Wanderer, just come back to me?

Soul Searching

When You Left Us

When you left us

The home you built for us became just a house

Warm laughter filled rooms

Echoed with silence, cold and hollow

When you left us

The links that had kept us together

Now lay broken in pieces

Scattered, never again to ever gather

When you left us

Relationships seemingly strong

Showed hidden weakness

Moving swiftly on not wanting to belong

When you left us

We prayed that we would one day meet again

To share memories of time spent apart

And live together, never to separate again

About the Author

Although Shaheen Darr's family originated from South Asia, she was born in Kenya. She left her home country to live her married life in Britain. A mother of three daughters, Darr describes them as "independent spirits with generous natures who enrich my every living moment."

Shaheen Darr has a background in business and finance, but writing fiction and poetry interest her the most.

She questions life continuously, and, finally, the whys and ifs from the pages of her diary were self-published in two books: **Soul Searching** and **The Spectrum of Life**. Her works include reflections on her main passions: love, life lessons, and nature. She says, "Nature relaxes and grounds me while nurturing my creative side."

Her latest release, **Kismet,** is a fiction novel loosely based on her own experiences of British life as an Asian woman.

Ms. Darr says, "I am excited about this journey into self-publishing, but I know that success lies in the support of people around me who have similar dreams. I hope those who read my books will enjoy my thoughts and reflections as much as I enjoyed writing them. Please feel free to e-mail me your comments or suggestions at **snowbrrd19@aol.com**. I will be happy to respond."